The front cover

This is a scene from the computer game.

What do you think the game involves?

Who do you think are the bad characters?

The title page

Which characters are the Quorks?

How do you know?

Read the names of the author and illustrator.

The back cover

Let's read the blurb together.

What do you think might go wrong?

LESSON 1 (Chapter 1)

Read pages 2 to 5

READ

Purpose: to confirm which are the bad characters and which ones the boys are defending.

Pause at page 5

EXPLORE

How are the Pods described in the story?

How would you describe the Quorks in your own words?

Why did the boys choose this game?

Chapter 1

Nick and Jonathan loved playing computer games.

"That's the one I want!" said Jonathan, pointing to the computer game in the shop window.

"*Quork Attack*," said Nick, reading the box. "I've heard that's great!"

"Come on," said Jonathan. "Let's go in and buy it!"

The shop was full of games, but *Quork Attack* definitely looked the most exciting. The boys hurried back to Jonathan's house with the game, eager to try it out.

As soon as they got back, they raced up to Jonathan's bedroom. While Jonathan loaded the game, Nick took a long look at the box.

The box was covered with pictures of blue and red creatures, zapping each other. The Pods were bright blue, potato-shaped creatures with powerful slime-rays. Their enemies, the Quorks, were small, red creatures with ten long spikes for legs. They looked really nasty.

"OK, I've loaded it," said Jonathan. "Are you ready to play?"

"Let's go!" said Nick, taking a seat next to him at the computer. Nick felt a tingling thrill at the back of his neck, as he always did when he was about to play a new game. You never knew quite what to expect!

READ

Read pages 6 to 8

Purpose: To find out what goes wrong.

EXPLORE

Pause at page 8

What did the boys discover as they played the game?

What did Jonathan think was wrong? What words are used to describe his feelings? (*strange, weird*)

What has happened to the Pods?

The boys played all afternoon, helping the Pods defend their planet from the horrible Quorks. They found it much harder than they thought it would be. No matter what they did, the Pods were being wiped out very quickly.

"I don't understand it!" said Jonathan in despair. "Nothing we do seems to make any difference."

"I know," said Nick. "Usually we get better at these games, not worse!"

Jonathan tried so hard to help the Pods that he began to really hate the Quorks. Then he started to have strange feelings about the Pods – it was as if they were too sad and weak to help themselves.

"This might sound weird," said Jonathan, "but it's almost like the Pods don't want to fight!"

"Don't be silly, Jonathan," said Nick. "It's only a game. No one gets hurt. It's not real. Quorks and Pods don't have feelings!"

"I said it would sound weird!" said Jonathan.

"Oh, I give up," said Nick, half an hour later. "I think there's something wrong with this game!"

"Come on," said Jonathan. "Let's get a drink, and then we'll play one more game."

"OK, just one more game and then I'm going home."

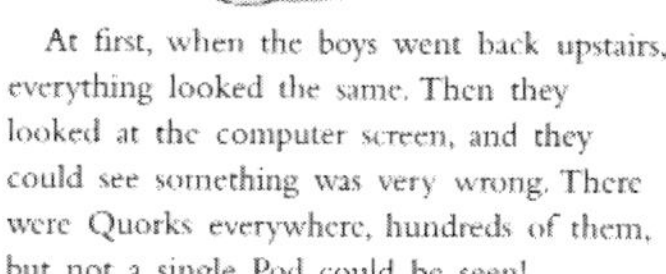

At first, when the boys went back upstairs, everything looked the same. Then they looked at the computer screen, and they could see something was very wrong. There were Quorks everywhere, hundreds of them, but not a single Pod could be seen!

Not one!

Read pages 10 and 11

READ

Purpose: To find out what has happened to the Pods.

Pause at page 11

EXPLORE

What evidence do the boys have that the Pods have escaped from the computer?

How do Nick and Jonathan feel? What words or phrases tell you? (*frightened, searched … frantically, totally confused*)

What would you do if you were Jonathan?

*Please turn to page 14 for **Revisit and Respond** activities.*

"Where are all the Pods?" asked Jonathan, clicking the computer mouse. "We can't have lost them all! Where can they be?"

"Maybe they've escaped!" joked Nick.

Nick looked at Jonathan and saw he wasn't laughing. "What's the matter?" Nick said, frowning. "It was only a joke!"

"Look!" said Jonathan, pointing to the floor.

"Where?" said Nick.

"There on the floor!" Jonathan whispered.

Nick looked down. "They look exactly like tiny slime-rays," he said with a gasp.

"Exactly," whispered Jonathan. "It's not a joke, Nick. The Pods really *have* escaped, and they've dropped their slime-rays."

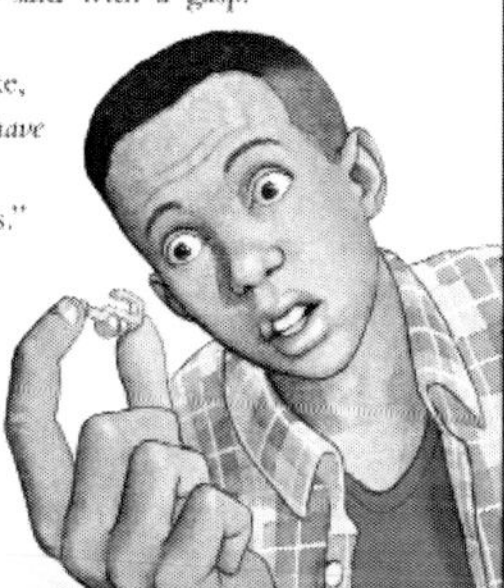

"What do we do now?" asked Nick. He was beginning to feel frightened.

"I don't know," said Jonathan, "but I *do* know we have to find those Pods."

Nick and Jonathan searched the room frantically, but they didn't find a single Pod.

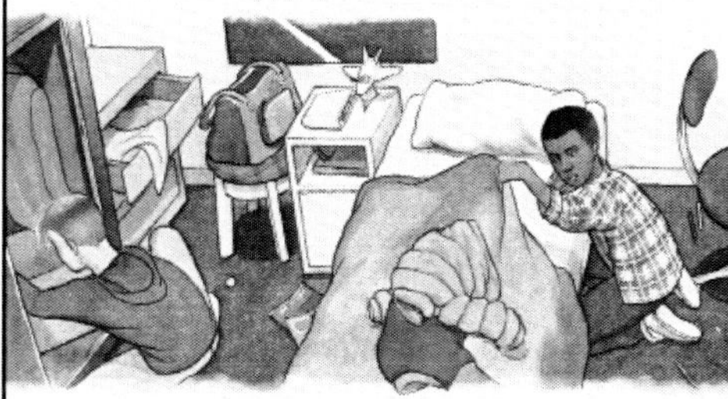

After a while, it was time for Nick to go home. Jonathan felt totally confused.

"I think I'll stop looking," he said.

Maybe they'd just played too many computer games.

LESSON 2 (Chapter 2)

Recap lesson 1

What type of story is *Quork Attack?* (*Remind the children that it is a mystery story as well as a science-fiction story.*)

What is the mystery? Where do you think the Pods might be?

Read pages 12 to 15

Purpose: To confirm predictions.

Pause at page 15

What is the difference between the Pods in the night and their appearance in the morning?

What will Jonathan and Nick have to do to save the Pods?

Chapter 2

Jonathan woke up suddenly in the middle of
the night. At first he didn't know what had
woken him. Then he heard something.
It was a small, muffled, bleeping sound, like
someone crying into a pillow.

Jonathan looked around in the dark, trying
to find where the noise was coming from.
That was when he saw the light. A bright
blue light was coming from the front pocket
of his school bag.

Quietly, Jonathan got out of bed, tiptoed
over to the bag, and peered into the pocket.
There were all the Pods, huddled together,
and bleeping softly.

"It's OK," Jonathan whispered. "I'm not
going to hurt you!"
The bleeping suddenly stopped, as if the
Pods understood.

"You'll be safe with me," said Jonathan,
quickly zipping up the pocket so they
couldn't escape again.

"I'll decide what to do with you in the
morning, when Nick comes before school."

Jonathan could hardly sleep for the rest of
the night.

The next morning, Jonathan showed Nick
where the Pods were hiding.

"They look very pale," said Nick, as he
peered into the pocket. "I thought the Pods
were bright blue."

"That's odd," said Jonathan. "They were
bright blue last night. Do you think they
might be sick?"

Nick put his hand into the pocket and
scooped out some of the Pods. He looked at
them, pale and weak in his hand.

"I think it's worse than that," said Nick.
"I think they're dying!"

Read pages 16 to 18

READ

Purpose: To find out what other problems the boys have.

Pause at page 18

EXPLORE

What two problems do the boys now have?

How will the boys stop the Quorks coming out of the screen?

What would you do to save the Pods?

"Maybe they can't survive for long outside
a computer," said Nick.

"I think you're right," said Jonathan as he
loaded the game again. "The sooner we get
them back on here, the better!"

"No," said Nick, "We can't! They haven't
got their slime-rays. They won't survive
without them!"

"I thought you were the one who said
they weren't real. You said it was just a
game," said Jonathan. "Now I don't know
what to do," he said in despair. "If we put
them back, they'll die. If we *don't* put them
back, they'll die!"

Nick wasn't listening. He was pointing at
the computer screen.

"Look!" he said, with a gasp.

Jonathan spun around to see what was
happening. The Quorks had stopped running
around and were all huddled together in one
corner of the screen.

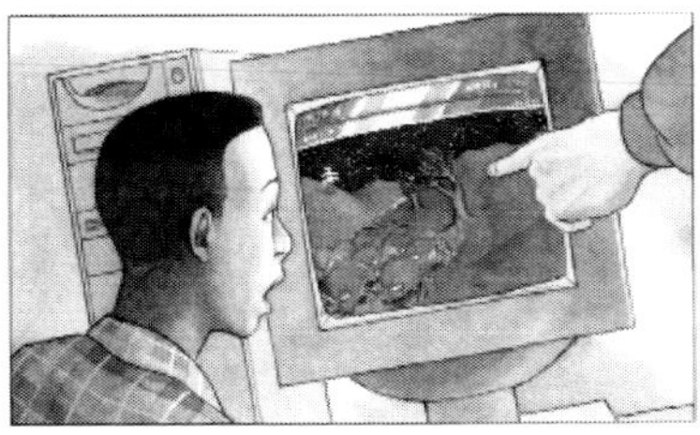

"What are they doing?" asked Nick.

"I don't know," said Jonathan.

Then suddenly, the tip of one long, thin,
red leg started to come through the screen.

"Oh, no! Quick!" yelled Nick.

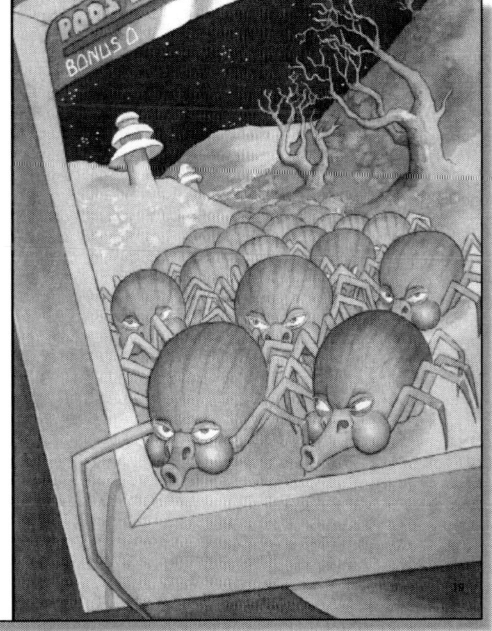

Read pages 20 to the end

Purpose: To find out how the boys saved the Pods.

Pause at page 24

Why were the Pods getting paler and paler?

Do you think the boys did the right thing?

How did they feel at the end?

Do you think the boys will buy any more computer games?

"Quick!" said Nick, as Jonathan put a blank disk into the computer.

"Ready," said Jonathan.

Nick held the Pods up to the screen and one by one they jumped back through it.

The screen flashed twice and then lots of bright blue Pods appeared. They were grinning and bleeping happily. Nick and Jonathan jumped for joy.

"We did it! We saved them!" shouted Nick.

Then the screen went blank for a second and a message appeared.

"So are we!" Nick and Jonathan said together.

"The only place this is going now is in the bin!" said Jonathan, throwing away the game.

"Absolutely!" said Nick with a grin.

After Reading
Revisit and Respond

Lesson 1

- What type of story do you think this is? (*science-fiction; mystery*) What mystery do the boys have to solve?

- What other mystery stories have you read? (*The Mystery Man*) What did Sam want to find out in *The Mystery Man?* How is *Quork Attack* similar to *The Mystery Man?* How is it different?

- Brainstorm different words to describe the Pods and the Quorks.

Lesson 2

- Look again at the ending of the story. Do you think the boys' problems are over for good? (*Prompt children to look at the illustration on page 24.*) What might the next mystery be?

- How does this ending compare with that of *The Mystery Man*? (*Sam starts to imagine new mysteries about the animals at the shelter.*) Why do you think some mystery stories end with a twist like this?

- Ask the children to decide which mystery story they liked best and why.

Follow-up
Independent Group Activity Work

This book is accompanied by two photocopy masters, one with a reading focus, and one with a writing focus, which support the teaching objectives of this book. The photocopy masters can be found in the *Planning and Assessment Guide.*

PCM F8.1 *(reading)*

PCM F8.2 *(writing)*

You may also like to invite the children to read the text again during their independent reading (either at school or at home).

Writing

Guided writing: Write a short review of *Quork Attack* using PCM F8.2.

Extended writing: Write your own mystery story about a computer game. What will the problem be? How will it be solved? Think of a good title for your story.

Assessment Points

Assess that the children have learnt the main teaching points of the book by checking that they can:

- explain their reactions to texts, commenting on important aspects (e.g. 'What would you do to save the Pods?').